DALÍ

Cossetània
EDICIONS

FIGUERES

1904

Salvador Dalí is the son of the notary public from Figueres. However, from a very early age he is sure he does not want to follow the family business. He wants to do something different: drawing. He always has a pencil in his hand and it is very soon clear that he has an extraordinary talent. Everyone is convinced he will become a great painter!

MADRID

1922-1926

When the time comes to study, Dalí enrols at
the San Fernando Royal Academy of Fine
Arts. There he shows that not only does he
have talent, he also has a wild character.
When the final exams arrive he does not
turn up. "The teachers are not worthy of my
genius," he says.

LORCA AND BUÑUEL

◆

In Madrid he wastes no time. At the
Students' Hall of Residence where he lives, he
makes friends with other artists, like Federico
García Lorca and Luis Buñuel. Together they
have a great time, but they also discover the
newest kind of art and help one another.
Later, Dalí and Buñuel will write the script
for the film *Un chien andalou*.

CADAQUÉS

1925

During his years of education, Dalí studies the classical painters, particularly Velàzquez, as well as modern painters, like Picasso. These influences will help him forge his own style. For the moment, he already has a great mastery of technique. This he demonstrates in the portrait he paints of his sister during the holidays: *Girl at the window*.

PARIS

1929

Dalí moves to Paris and joins the Surrealist group. This group, led by André Breton, is revolutionising art. Its members do not want to copy reality and instead give absolute free rein to the imagination. Thrilled by this atmosphere, Dalí creates the "paranoiac-critical" method, makes his moustache a badge of identity and develops a very personal painting style.

STYLE

In Dalí's style, fantasy has absolute freedom, as the surrealists would want. However, we also find many personal traits. Firstly, a technique so perfect that objects can almost be confused with photographs. Meanwhile, there are figures never seen before: melting clocks, long-legged elephants, telephones with lobsters and so on.

NEW YORK · CADAQUÉS · LONDON · PEQUÍN

GALA

1929-1982

In Paris, Dalí meets the surrealists, and also Gala. This Russian girl will become something more than a wife to him: she will be his accomplice. Together they will live at Portlligat and travel around the world. Gala will also be the model for pictures like *The Madonna of Portlligat.*

UNITED STATES

1934-1989

The United States is an important place for Dalí. The Americans love his work and there he will collaborate on films by Alfred Hitchcock and Walt Disney, among others. They also love his eccentricities, such as wondering every morning: "What wonderful things is this Salvador Dalí going to accomplish today?" While some consider him mad, Dalí firmly refutes them: "The only difference between me and a madman is that I'm not mad."

SCIENCE AND MYSTICISM

As he grows old, Dalí faithfully follows his style: always perfect and with unrestrained fantasy. But now he is evolving towards other themes, particularly science and mysticism. For Dalí they are related, allowing him to create works like *Christ of Saint John of the Cross*.

PORTLLIGAT

1949-1989

During his life, Dalí travels the world, where he is admired, but he finally decides to settle at Portlligat. Dalí lives in this small coastal village with Gala, painting a great deal of his work there. Only when he is very old does he return to Figueres, where he dies on 23 January 1989.

CHRONOLOGY

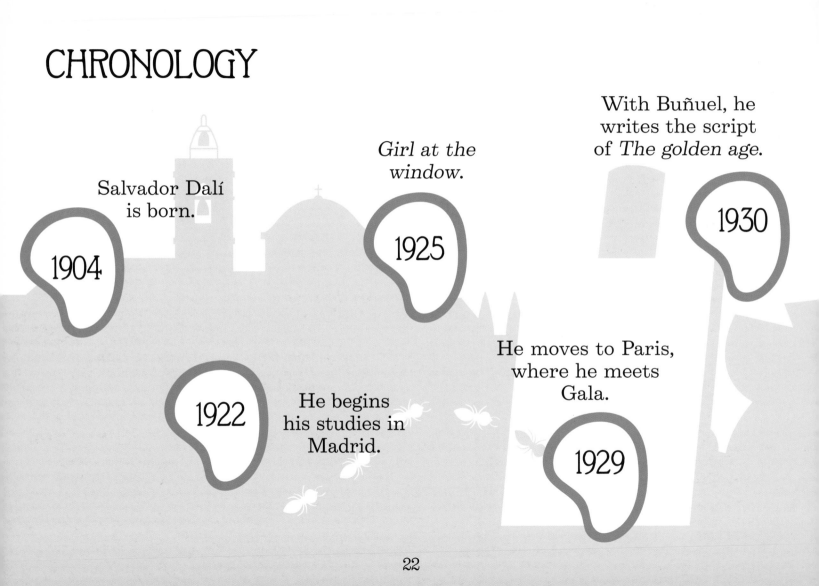

Salvador Dalí
is born.

1904

*Girl at the
window.*

1925

With Buñuel, he
writes the script
of *The golden age.*

1930

1922

He begins
his studies in
Madrid.

He moves to Paris,
where he meets
Gala.

1929

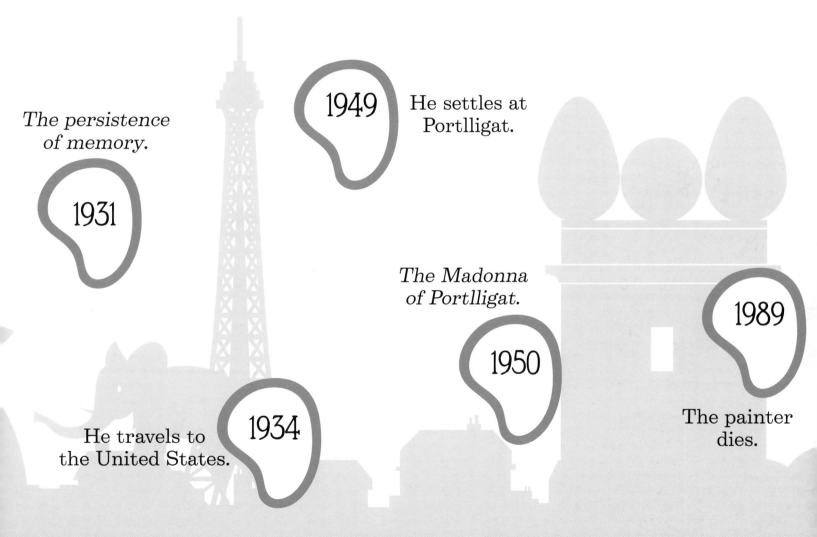

The persistence of memory.

1931

1949 He settles at Portlligat.

He travels to the United States. 1934

The Madonna of Portlligat.

1950

1989

The painter dies.

GALERÍA DE PERSONAJES

Conoce a algunos de los artistas más relevantes
en la vida y obra de Dalí

André Breton

A poet and novelist, Breton came
to be the father of surrealism.
Highlights of his work include
Manifestos of surrealism and the
novel *Nadja*, as well as books of
poems like *Soluble fish*. He
maintained an intense – and
tense – relationship with
Salvador Dalí.

Pablo Picasso

One of the great painters of the
20th-century avant-garde,
together with Dalí. Committed
to social causes, he was the
father of Cubism and the painter
of essential works like
Les demoiselles d'Avignon and
Guernica. Of him, Dalí said:
"Picasso is Spanish. Me too.
Picasso is a genius. Me too.
Picasso is a Communist. Me
neither."

Federico García Lorca

One of the great poets in Spanish
of the 20th century, he was author
of books of poems like *Poet in
New York*, and plays like *Yerma*.
He met Dalí in Madrid and was
the unwitting main character of
Un chien andalou.

Joan Miró

Another classic figure of surrealism. The paintings by this Barcelona-born artist are outstanding for their bright colours and abstract forms and they have evocative titles like *The Harlequin's carnival*, *Hands flying off toward the constellations* or *Women and bird in the moonlight*.

Man Ray

While many avant-garde art movements have a photographer, no other shares Surrealism's distinction in having Man Ray. This American's experimental techniques revolutionised the art of photography and changed the way we look at reality.

Luis Buñuel

Although they later fell out, Buñuel was one of the great friends of Salvador Dalí's youth. Together, they wrote the script for this film-maker's first film, *Un chien andalou*. Other films by Buñuel are *Viridiana* or *The discreet charm of the bourgeoisie*.

THE SEVEN DIFFERENCES

Find the seven differences.

WORDSEARCH

Find seven artists related to Dalí.

Z	A	M	O	D	E	Z	A	Ñ	G	L	E	S	L	S
D	P	I	C	A	S	S	O	A	A	O	W	G	A	L
A	P	R	R	K	J	A	K	P	L	Y	I	F	B	E
Y	I	O	R	A	E	M	A	T	O	G	J	Z	R	M
A	U	A	H	L	V	E	P	E	Ñ	M	O	A	E	A
S	O	Ñ	A	S	M	A	N	R	A	Y	S	W	T	B
E	F	I	T	J	P	I	N	L	E	P	Q	A	O	O
W	K	O	A	D	U	C	H	A	M	P	U	S	N	A
Y	A	G	S	W	E	L	F	Q	L	Ñ	Z	I	W	S
X	A	H	M	E	S	B	U	Ñ	U	E	L	T	O	L
C	R	E	V	G	A	W	H	R	E	O	U	Z	A	E
O	W	A	R	H	O	L	S	A	Y	A	Q	L	L	O
N	A	L	B	M	U	Q	E	G	E	M	I	D	A	Z

27

WHERE IS DALÍ?

Salvador Dalí has got lost in the San Fernando Academy of Fine Arts. Can you help find him? You will also find two birds, three square palettes, four artists with blue pencils and five tubes of oil paint.

THE EXACT TIME

Find the two clocks showing the same time!

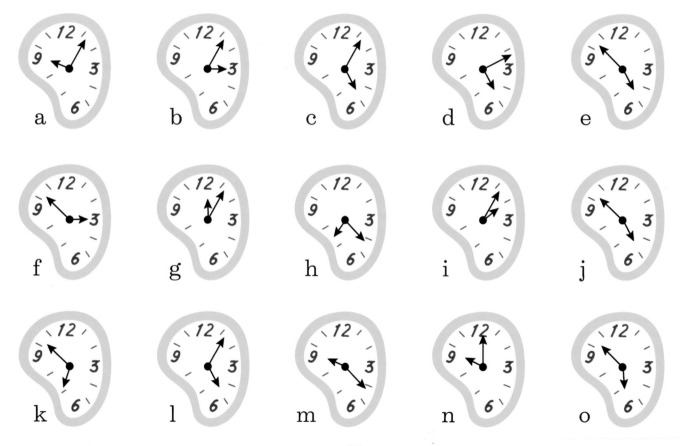

a b c d e

f g h i j

k l m n o

WHERE WAS DALÍ BORN?

a)   In Paris.

b)   In Figueres.

c)   In Barcelona.

d)   In Cadaqués.

First edition: March 2016

© on the text: Marià Veloy Planas
© on the illustrations: David Maynar Gálvez

© on this edition:
9 Grup Editorial
Cossetània Edicions
C/ Violeta, 6 - 43800 Valls
Tel. (34) 977 60 25 91
Fax (34) 977 61 43 57
cossetania@cossetania.com
www.cossetania.com

Translation: Simon Berrill

Design and layout: Imatge-9, SL

Printing: Leitzaran Grafikak

ISBN: 978-84-9034-413-2

DL T 204-2016

Every morning when he got up, Salvador Dalí asked himself the same question: "What wonderful things is this Salvador Dalí going to accomplish today?" And although some took him for mad, the fact is that he did do many wonderful things. Not only did he paint pictures today on display in museums all over the world, he also had a very exciting life. He fell hopelessly in love, he had friends who revolutionised art... and he triumphed in Hollywood. Would you like to know more? Have a look inside this book!

Cossetània EDICIONS

IBIC: YBCH, AB

9 788490 344132